ARCTIC

ARCTIC

LIFE INSIDE THE ARCTIC CIRCLE

CLAUDIA MARTIN

amber
BOOKS

Published by Amber Books Ltd
United House
North Road
London N7 9DP
United Kingdom
www.amberbooks.co.uk
Instagram: amberbooksltd
Facebook: amberbooks
Twitter: @amberbooks

ISBN: 978-1-83886-047-9

Project Editor: George Maudsley
Designer: Keren Harragan
Picture Research: Terry Forshaw

Printed in China

Contents

Introduction

One of the world's last remaining wildernesses, the Arctic is testament to life's determination to thrive against seemingly impossible odds: butterflies flutter across the tundra during the brief summer, long-haired muskoxen dig beneath the snow for plant shoots, Arctic societies work and bring up families in winter temperatures as low as -67°C (-89°F). Yet fears are growing that the odds against life in the Arctic may be rising too fast for this fragile ecosystem. The Arctic is particularly vulnerable to climate change, with modellers predicting warming above the global average. The Arctic Ocean sea ice, the Greenland ice sheet and the permafrost that underlies the tundra are all at risk of catastrophic thawing, perhaps destruction. The growing sense that the treasures of the Arctic may be about to slip away permanently has not only turned the eyes of the scientific community on the region but also encouraged a growing number of travellers to journey to this beautiful wilderness, hoping to glimpse a polar bear on the distant ice or to taste a cloudberry on the tundra, before it is too late.

ABOVE:
Caribou, Nunavut, Canada
Caribou, or reindeer, live across the Arctic region.

OPPOSITE:
Henry Kater Peninsula, Baffin Island, Canada
Cotton grass seed heads dot the summer tundra.

Arctic Lands

The Arctic Circle, around 66.6° north of the equator, runs through Iceland, Norway, Sweden, Finland, Russia, the US state of Alaska, Canada and Greenland – which is an autonomous territory within the Kingdom of Denmark. Land inside the Arctic Circle experiences cold winters and cool summers. Winters are dark, with snow and ice covering the ground. At this time, temperatures average below freezing over almost the whole region. During the brief summer, days are long, as the sun barely dips below the horizon. Average summer temperatures are above freezing in all Arctic lands, except the interior of Greenland. The world's second largest ice sheet, after that of Antarctica, is found here, covering 90 per cent of Greenland. Across the Arctic, higher elevations are permanently covered by snow or glacial ice. Elsewhere, tundra predominates, an ecosystem where trees cannot grow because of the cold and the short growing season, as well as the layer of permafrost, or permanently frozen soil, that prevents deep roots. Only such plants as low shrubs, mosses and lichens find the resources they need. As the tundra's top layer of soil melts in summer, the ground may become soggy. In the far south of the Arctic, the taiga begins, stretching southward and around the globe to form a band of forest where pines, spruces and larches dominate. Today, all these lands are severely affected by climate change, which is causing dramatic melting of the Greenland ice sheet and thawing of the permafrost.

LEFT:

Baffin Island, Nunavut, Canada
Canada's largest island is one of the 36,000 islets and islands of the Canadian Arctic Archipelago. Baffin's terrain is tundra, apart from among the glacier-covered mountains. Sea ice surrounds the coast for much of the year, disappearing from the northern coast only during high summer, when the temperature usually reaches no higher than 10°C (50°F).

Ellesmere Island, Nunavut, Canada
In Quttinirpaaq National Park, the Charybdis glacier almost touches noses with Scylla glacier (centre), the pair named after the sea monsters of Greek myth. In Inuktitut, Quttinirpaaq means 'top of the world', a suitable name for the world's second most northerly national park, after the Northeast Greenland National Park.

LEFT:

Wapusk National Park, Manitoba, Canada
On the shores of Hudson Bay, this national park lies in the transition zone between forest and tundra. The western Hudson Bay population of around a thousand polar bears roam here during summer and early autumn, waiting for the bay's sea ice to return.

RIGHT:

Ellesmere Island, Nunavut, Canada
The small community of Grise Fiord lies on mountainous Ellesmere Island, overlooking Jones Sound. With a population of around 130 and an average temperature of -16.5°C (3.2°F), the village is Canada's most northerly civilian settlement. It is connected to the rest of the world only by a dangerously mountain-fringed airstrip.

Campbell Lake, Northwest Territories, Canada
Not far from the town of Inuvik, Campbell Lake is in Gwich'in Territorial Park. It is the northernmost limit of plants such as aspen and lowbush cranberry. During the short summer season, the park is visited by kayakers, birdwatchers and campers. The Dempster Highway provides access to Inuvik, other than during the freeze-up and thaw of the Mackenzie River, when it cannot be crossed by either ferry or ice bridge.

LEFT:

Buchan Gulf, Baffin Island, Nunavut, Canada
On Baffin Island's northeastern coast, this fjord was carved
between steep cliffs that reach 600m (1970ft) above sea level.
Northern fulmars can be seen nesting on rock ledges from
early April to late September, while narwhals and walruses
swim through the icy water.

ABOVE:

Coast of Banks Island, Northwest Territories, Canada
Surrounded by sea ice for much of the year, Banks Island was
named in honour of naturalist Joseph Banks in 1820. The only
settlement on the island is Sachs Harbour, home to around 100
people who live mostly by hunting, trapping and catering to
the tourists who visit the island's Aulavik National Park.

Iceberg off the coast of Newfoundland, Canada
Every year, large icebergs calve from the glaciers of the Canadian Arctic and Greenland, then float southward into the Atlantic Ocean, finally melting off the coast of Newfoundland and Labrador. Along the coast of Newfoundland, icebergs are best viewed in late May and early June; off Labrador, they can be seen between March and July. As climate change accelerates, larger icebergs pass the region in greater numbers.

FAR RIGHT:
Sea ice off Baffin Island, Nunavut, Canada
While some sea ice in the Canadian Arctic melts and freezes annually (called first-year ice), some ice remains year round (called multi-year ice). The waters of the Canadian Arctic Archipelago, Beaufort Sea and Kane Basin retain a region of sea ice year round, but this multi-year ice has been decreasing over the last 50 years as a result of rising global temperatures.

Fitzroy glacier, Devon Island, Nunavut, Canada
At 55,247 sq km (21,331 sq miles), Devon Island is the world's largest uninhabited island. The Fitzroy glacier is one of several belonging to the Devon ice cap, which covers 14,000 sq km (5,400 sq miles). The island's almost barren Haughton Crater is considered a similar landscape to that of Mars, leading to the establishment of a NASA research base.

Kivalliq Region, Nunavut, Canada
While the southerly reaches of Nunavut experience a subarctic climate, much of continental Nunavut has a tundra climate. In this zone, while at least one month has an average temperature above freezing, no month has an average temperature higher than 10°C (50°F). Although no trees can grow, specialized plants can survive, such as Arctic cotton, Lapland rosebay and purple saxifrage.

Kivalliq Region, Nunavut, Canada
In the featureless tundra, Inuit communities traditionally build stone cairns, called *inuksuit*, as navigation tools or markers for hunting and camping grounds. *Inuksuk* comes from the Inuktitut for 'acting in the capacity of a human'. Today, *inuksuit* are an Inuit cultural symbol. The flag of the territory of Nunavut features a red *inuksuk* on a yellow and white background.

Lapland, Finland
The northernmost region of
Finland, Lapland is known
as Sápmi to the Sámi. The
winters are long here, with
snow covering the ground
between November and April.
Apart from in the far north,
much of the land is covered
by coniferous forest.

Northern lights, Lapland, Finland
In northern Lapland, the northern lights can be seen on clear nights between September and March. The lights are caused by the solar wind, which passes on energy to gases in Earth's atmosphere, which release that energy as light. Earth's magnetic field guides the solar wind towards the poles.

Muonio River, Lapland, Finland
The Tornio River and its tributary, the Muonio, form the national boundary between Finland and Sweden. This border was fixed in the 1809 Treaty of Fredrikshamn, which split Lapland between Sweden and Finland, then the Russian Grand Duchy of Finland.

Lapland, Finland
In February, the coldest month, the temperature in Lapland can dip to -30°C (-22°F) but usually hovers around -10°C (14°F). Low-lying areas are covered by bogs, while pines and spruces cloak the low fells. The tops of the fells, typically no more than 1300m (4265ft) above sea level, are usually treeless.

Riisitunturi National Park, Lapland, Finland
In winter, the spruce trees that crowd many of Riisitunturi National Park's hillsides are coated with layer after layer of frost, weighing down their branches and creating otherworldly shapes. The park also encompasses countless swamps, including rare hillside ones.

Northern Lapland, Finland
Home to only around three per cent of Finland's people but the country's largest region, Lapland is the least densely populated area in mainland Europe. The municipality with fewest people here is Savukoski, in northeastern Lapland, which has only 0.16 inhabitants per 1 sq km (0.41 per 1 sq mile). According to Finnish folklore, a number of those inhabitants are Santa Claus and his elves.

**Iceberg, Disko Bay,
Greenland**
Disko Bay is at the western
end of the Ilulissat Icefjord,
which runs eastward to the
vast Greenland ice sheet.
Here the fjord meets the
Jakobshavn glacier, which
flows at up to 35m (115ft) per
day, resulting in the annual
calving of around 20 billion
tonnes of icebergs, which
float out into the bay.

Kangerlussuatsiaq Fjord, Greenland
Known in Danish as Evighedsfjorden ('Eternity Fjord'), this fjord is 75km (47 miles) long and up to 700m (2300ft) deep. The fjord drains the Maniitsoq ice cap, which is now separated from the Greenland ice sheet by a narrow valley. The mountains surrounding the fjord are Greenland's premier destination for heliskiing and climbing.

Sun halo, Greenland
Sun halos are caused by ice crystals in the atmosphere, which refract the sun's light. This type of halo is known as a 22° halo, as no light is refracted at an angle smaller than 22°, making the sky darker inside the ring. Halos formed by low-level ice crystals are more common in polar regions.

LEFT:

Iceberg, Greenland
Greenlanders have traditionally used the appearance of icebergs to distinguish the seasons and as landmarks, a testament to the endurance of these sculptural features of the seascape. The icebergs, made of frozen freshwater, calve from the many glaciers that stretch to the island's fjords, with iceberg hubs being the Ilulissat Icefjord on the west coast and the Sermilik Fjord on the east. The coast of southern Greenland is also known for its large sheets of floating sea ice.

RIGHT:

Helheim glacier, Greenland
Helheim glacier calves into Helheim Fjord, a branch of the Sermilik Fjord system. In Greenlandic, Sermilik means 'place with glaciers'. Helheim, named after the world of the dead in Norse mythology, is one of the fastest-flowing glaciers in Greenland, moving at up to 11km (6.8 miles) per year.

Scoresby Sund, Greenland
The longest fjord in the world, Scoresby Sund (known as Kangertittivaq in Greenlandic) stretches inland for 350km (216 miles). The whole fjord system covers an area of around 38,000 sq km (14,700 sq miles) of Greenland's southeastern corner. The fjord system was first mapped by the English explorer William Scoresby in 1822.

LEFT:

Tundra, Ilulissat, Greenland

As the temperature falls, the autumn tundra is a colourful patchwork of mosses, mushrooms and ferns. Their flowers gone, tufted saxifrage and Labrador tea still form thick mats. Thickets of Arctic willow line rivers and streams, while rocks are covered by orange, yellow, black or white lichens.

RIGHT:

Cloudberries

Able to survive as far north as 78°, cloudberries grow wild in Arctic, subarctic and mountainous temperate regions. The pink-gold fruits are a delicacy in Scandinavia, as well as a staple food of Alaska's Yup'ik, who use them as an ingredient in *akutaq*. Also known as 'Alaskan ice cream', this traditional dish contains berries, fish, tundra greens and animal fat.

LEFT:

Kirkjufell, Iceland

This 463m (1,519ft) high mountain, on the north coast of Iceland's Snæfellsnes peninsula, found wider fame from 2016, when it became 'Arrowhead Mountain' in seasons six and seven of *Game of Thrones*. Kirkjufell ('Church Mountain') is a *nunatak*, a high rock that has been left standing after glaciers eroded the surrounding land.

RIGHT:

Arctic Henge, Raufarhöfn, Iceland

This monument, begun in 1996, is designed to act as a vast sundial and calendar as it captures the sun's rays and shadows through its gateways, in a similar manner to England's Stonehenge. The monument was inspired by the tenth-century Icelandic poem *Völuspá*, which tells the story of the creation of the world and its coming end. The monument's 72 small blocks represent the 72 dwarves of the poem, which signified the seasons.

Svinafellsjökull glacier, Iceland

In Vatnajökull National Park, Svinafellsjökull is a tongue of Iceland's largest ice cap, Vatnajökull, which covers 7900 sq km (3050 sq miles). There are several volcanoes under the ice cap, which can cause dangerous *jökulhlaups* (glacial lake outburst floods) whenever they erupt. Svinafellsjökull's deeply crevassed body is too unstable for people to walk on, but was used in the television series *Game of Thrones* to represent landscapes 'north of the Wall'.

Jökulsárlón, Iceland
This large glacial lake, in Vatnajökull National Park, was formed by the melt from the Breiðamerkurjökull glacier in 1934–35. The lake has quadrupled in size since the 1970s as the glacier has retreated from the coast. It is now the deepest lake in Iceland, reaching 284m (932ft). Glaciologists think it probable that a deep fjord will eventually be worn on the site of the lake.

Hamnøy, Lofoten Islands, Norway
The fishing hamlet of Hamnøy is on Moskenesøya, near the southern end of the Lofoten archipelago, which experiences a relatively mild climate for its latitude thanks to the Gulf Stream. The traditional red *rorbu* houses hang over the rocks or water, one end propped on poles, for easy access to boats.

Spitsbergen, Svalbard archipelago, Norway
Spitsbergen is the largest and only permanently inhabited island of the Svalbard archipelago, which lies about 1050km (650 miles) from the North Pole. The high land in the island's interior is permanently covered by ice, but favourable winds keep the west coast fjords navigable for most of the year.

**Skagsanden beach,
Lofoten Islands, Norway**
This golden sand beach on
Flakstadøya is renowned for
the rippling patterns made
by a stream as it flows over
the shore to the sea. Since the
beach faces northwestward, it
is an ideal spot for watching
the northern lights.

LEFT:

Flakstadøya, Lofoten Islands, Norway

The best months for viewing the northern lights on the Lofoten Islands are October, February and early March. Although there is sufficient darkness for the lights to be seen by late afternoon, the most spectacular displays are usually between 8pm or 9pm and midnight. During the height of winter, the weather may be too stormy to get a clear view.

RIGHT:

Myrland, Flakstadøya, Lofoten Islands, Norway

The beach at Myrland (meaning 'peat land') overlooks the Nappstraumen Strait, on the other side of which is the island of Vestvagøya. Peaks of glacially eroded granite and gneiss plunge into the sea, which has a surface temperature of between 4°C (39°F) and a relatively warm 15°C (59°F), during July.

LEFT:

Spitsbergen, Svalbard archipelago, Norway
Near Spitsbergen's main settlement of Longyearbyen, along the Isfjord, are many flat-topped *nunataks*, worn away by countless glaciers. This is the warmest and wettest part of the entire archipelago, lying at the meeting point of mild, humid air from the south and cold air travelling from the north.

BELOW:

Trollfjord, Austvågøya, Lofoten Islands, Norway
Fringed by mountains up to 1100m (3600ft) high, this fjord is named after the evil trolls of Norse mythology, which were said to turn to stone if exposed to sunlight. In 1890, the fjord was the scene of a battle over fishing rights between industrial, steam-driven ships and traditional open-boat fishermen.

LEFT:

Austfonna ice cap, Nordaustlandet, Svalbard archipelago, Norway

Austfonna is the third largest ice cap in Europe, after the Severny Island ice cap of Novaya Zemlya, Russia, and Iceland's Vatnajökull. Austfonna covers 7800 sq km (3000 sq miles), more than half of the island of Nordaustlandet. An ice wall up to 20m (65ft) high calves into the Arctic Ocean.

RIGHT:

Sea ice, Svalbard archipelago, Norway

At its winter peak, the Arctic sea ice stretches just to the eastern coasts of Svalbard. Since 1970, the average winter temperature on the archipelago has risen by more than 7°C (12°F). And since 1979, the Arctic sea ice has shrunk by nearly 12 per cent each decade, with the greatest winter reduction in the Svalbard and Barents Sea region.

Hail storm, Flakstadøya, Lofoten Islands, Norway
Although summers are mild in the Lofoten archipelago, late autumn brings storms, snow, hail, sleet and rain. In some winters, snowfall on the mountains is heavy, raising the risk of avalanches. Temperatures below -10°C (14°F) are uncommon, even on the darkest winter days, but the islands' strong winds can be bitterly chilling. By April, the islands are thawing, although storms and sudden snow flurries can still take travellers by surprise.

57

A storm clears over Spitsbergen, Svalbard archipelago, Norway

Spitsbergen is the meeting point for cold polar air and warmer, moister air from the south, resulting in high winds and sudden, dangerous storms, even during the summer. The lowest temperature ever recorded on the archipelago was -46.3°C (-51.3°F), but the winter low is more commonly around -20°C (-4°F). During the long, pale summer days, the average high is 7°C (44.6°F).

High waves, Arctic Ocean

The coldest of the oceans, the Arctic has a surface temperature of around -1.8°C (28.8°F), close to the freezing point of saltwater. The ocean is the breeding ground of fierce Arctic storms, also called polar cyclones, which are low-pressure systems in which the air spins anticlockwise. Climate change is increasing the number of storms, which are contributing to the break-up of sea ice as they stir up warmer water.

Franz Josef Land, Russia
Around 260km (160 miles) east of the Norwegian Svalbard archipelago, Franz Josef Land consists of 192 islands that are scattered over a vast swathe of ocean, stretching for 375km (233 miles) west to east. Inhabited only by Russian military personnel, the archipelago sees very few tourists, who usually travel by icebreaker from Murmansk, Russia.

Laptev Sea coast, Russia
The Laptev Sea stretches northward from the coast of Siberia. This sea, far removed from the warming Atlantic or Pacific, has the most extreme climate of any Arctic sea. For about eight months of the year, its waters are covered by ice. In August, the coast may, very rarely, warm to as much as 34°C (93°F), yet sudden snow storms can strike even during the summer.

LEFT:

Eastern Chukotka, Russia

Chukotka Autonomous Okrug, the northeasternmost region of Russia, is mountainous and sparsely populated. About half the region lies north of the Arctic Circle, its coastal Arctic desert meeting the East Siberian and Chukchi Seas. Tundra covers the centre of the region, while taiga cloaks the south. Anadyr, the administrative centre of Chukotka, is the most easterly settlement with town status in Russia.

RIGHT:

Chukchi Peninsula, Chukotka, Russia

Asia's easternmost peninsula plunges into the Bering Strait just 82km (51 miles) from Cape Prince of Wales in Alaska. Genetic analysis has shown that the Chukchi indigenous people are the closest Asian relatives of the indigenous societies of the Americas.

Waring Point, Wrangel Island, Chukotka, Russia
Around 140km (87 miles) from the Siberian coast, Wrangel Island was the last known home of woolly mammoths, which survived here until 2500–2000 BC. The island is a meeting point for Arctic and Pacific air masses, resulting in high winds and fogs. Waring Point is known for its large nesting colonies of horned and tufted puffins, thick-billed murres and glaucous gulls.

BELOW:

Teshekpuk Lake Wetlands, Alaska, USA
This area is a thermokarst wetland, characterized by lakes and marshy hollows formed as the permafrost thaws in summer. The wetland is home to barren-ground caribou, as well as being a moulting ground for tens of thousands of greater white-fronted, brant, Canada and snow geese.

RIGHT:

Dalton Highway, North Slope, Alaska, USA
Since 1974, the Dalton Highway has run 666km (414 miles) from Fairbanks, in central Alaska, to Deadhorse, on the Arctic Ocean's Prudhoe Bay. Famous for being a hair-raising drive, the road has had various features names by truckers: 'Oil Spill Hill', 'Oh Shit Corner' and the 'Roller Coaster'.

LEFT:

North Slope, Brooks Range, Alaska, USA

The Brooks Range stretches for 1100km (680 miles) across the state of Alaska and into Canada's Yukon territory. The northern treeline always ran through these mountains, with only the occasional stand of balsam poplar, trembling aspen and white spruce on the tundra of the North Slope beyond. Rising temperatures, however, are seeing such trees as black spruce advance slowly beyond the mountains.

RIGHT:

Gates of the Arctic National Park, Alaska, USA

The Tinayguk River meanders through a broad glacial valley in Gates of the Arctic National Park, the most northerly and least visited national park in the United States. The roadless park encompasses the Brooks Range's Endicott Mountains, forests of spruce and poplar and, to the north, vast swathes of tundra. The long winters reach -59°C (-74°F), but the temperature can soar to 32°C (90°F) in the short, sudden summer.

LEFT:
Point Barrow, Alaska, USA
Point Barrow, or Nuvuk, is the northernmost point of the United States, 2078km (1291 miles) from the North Pole. This scrap of land is the dividing point between the Beaufort and Chukchi seas. The water is ice-free only in summer.

ABOVE:
Deadhorse, Prudhoe Bay, Alaska, USA
The town of Deadhorse is populated by workers at the Prudhoe Bay oil field. The town probably gets its name from the Dead Horse Haulers trucking company, which was a major employer in the area during the 1960s and 1970s.

Wildlife of the Arctic

Life in the Arctic is bitterly hard, with low temperatures, fierce storms and long, dark winters, when food on land is scarce. Such conditions have not led to biodiversity in the Arctic, where just five species of amphibians and a couple of reptiles exist. The animals that do survive the far north have developed extraordinary adaptations, from the long, warm fur of the muskox to the thick fat of the beluga whale. To escape the Arctic winter, Arctic birds and many marine mammals undertake lengthy seasonal migrations. Of the animals that remain through winter, many hibernate beneath the soil or snow. Others, such as the Svalbard reindeer, stay above ground but move so slowly that they are able to survive on their reserves through the winter night.

These defences, developed over millions of years, are no match for the sudden challenges of climate change. The warming of the Arctic Ocean is, year by year, shrinking the sea ice and shortening the season when it remains a strong enough platform for hunting polar bears or resting bearded seals. On land, the Arctic tundra is retreating, with the treeline edging northward, shrubs and trees displacing moss and lichen. Likewise, animals of the subarctic region are moving northward, putting pressure on tundra species. The Arctic fox is a victim of such a northward spread by the red fox. In addition, the tundra is seeing far higher winter rainfall, which freezes into a layer of ice that locks plants out of the reach of herbivores, threatening such iconic Arctic residents as caribou.

LEFT:
Polar Bear, Svalbard archipelago, Norway
Polar bears are marine mammals that spend most of their life on the sea ice of the Arctic Ocean, hunting for seals, their favourite prey. When the sea ice melts in summer, most bears move inland, sometimes being seen as far south as Canada's Newfoundland. The polar bear's range includes Greenland, the Svalbard archipelago, northern Russia, Alaska and Canada.

Polar bear, Svalbard archipelago, Norway
Polar bears usually catch seals when they surface for air at breathing holes in the ice. The bears use their short, strong claws to grab and drag out their heavy prey. Polar bears' feet are wide, up to 30cm (12in) across, to distribute their weight when walking on snow or thin ice, as well as to act as paddles when swimming.

LEFT:

**Polar bear,
Thorland, Greenland**
Polar bears can swim for
many days at a time, moving
in a doggie-paddle fashion
with a thick layer of fat to
keep them warm and provide
buoyancy. Their top known
swimming speed is 10km/h
(6mph). Polar bears are
also known to make short
underwater dives, probably
no deeper than 6m (20ft)
and not lasting longer than
three minutes. While
underwater, the bears'
nostrils close.

RIGHT:

**Polar bear, Churchill,
Manitoba, Canada**
The town of Churchill is
famous for the many hungry
polar bears that pass through
in autumn, heading for the
refreezing Hudson Bay. Bears
that persistently loiter in
town may be moved to the
Polar Bear Holding Facility
until the sea ice is ready for
them. Travellers can take
polar bear viewing trips on
the surrounding tundra using
modified vehicles.

LEFT:

Bearded seal, Svalbard archipelago, Norway

Bearded seals are named for their long, bristly whiskers. These are the largest Arctic seals, up to 2.7m (8.8ft) long and weighing up to 430kg (950lb). Along with ringed seals, they are heavily preyed on by polar bears. Bearded seals are found in coastal Arctic waters, as well as along the far northern coasts of the Atlantic and Pacific oceans. These seals climb on to sea ice to give birth to pups and to rest between trips to find clams, squid and fish near or on the seafloor.

BELOW:

Polar bear, Svalbard archipelago, Norway

While its major food source is seals, polar bears are also known to eat young walruses and dead, washed-up whales. When bears move on to land during the summer and early autumn, they eat whatever is available, from berries, roots and eggs to birds, rodents and reindeer. Rising temperatures are causing the sea ice to melt earlier in the year, forcing bears inland before they have built large enough fat reserves to survive the period of scarce food before the sea ice refreezes.

LEFT:

**Arctic hare,
Baffin Island, Canada**

This thickly furred hare, with short limbs and ears for warmth, is found on the coasts of Greenland, in the Canadian Arctic Archipelago and in northeastern continental Canada. In the southern reaches of its range, the hare moults its white fur in summer, growing brown to grey hair. Further north, where summers are very short, it stays white throughout the year.

RIGHT:

Alaska moose, Alaska, USA

Known as the Yukon moose in Canada, this large moose lives in taiga and deciduous forests in Alaska and Canada's Yukon territory. A mature bull moose can grow antlers up to 2.1m (6.9ft) across. Antlers are used in dominance displays and fights with rival males. After the mating season, males drop their antlers to save energy during winter.

LEFT:

Muskrat, Canada
This semi-aquatic rodent is native to northern North America and has been introduced to northern Eurasia. The muskrat does not hibernate in winter. When the ground is covered by snow and ice, it must search underwater for plants to eat; it does so by making holes in the frozen water surface with its sharp teeth.

BELOW LEFT:

Moor frog, Finland
The moor frog is one of only five amphibians (three other frogs, plus the Siberian newt) that are found north of the Arctic Circle. Its range spreads from Central Europe to Central Asia and includes such diverse habitats as tundra, forest and steppe. In the far north, these frogs hibernate between September and June.

RIGHT:

Beluga whale, Somerset Island, Nunavut, Canada
This Arctic and subarctic cetacean is well adapted to life in ice-covered seas, with its white skin and lack of a dorsal fin, which allows it to swim close under sea ice. Up to half the beluga's bodyweight is fat for keeping it warm, which serves as a fuel reserve. The beluga's large melon, the mass of adipose tissue on its forehead, is used for echolocation, modulating the whale's vocalizations.

LEFT:

**Siberian husky,
Murmansk Oblast, Russia**
Believed to have been bred
as sled dogs by the Chukchi
people of northeastern
Siberia, these hardy, thick-
coated dogs can withstand
temperatures as low as -60°C
(-76°F). Huskies have a strong
pack mentality and a high
prey drive (desire to pursue
and catch prey), but are not
usually territorial. Most
huskies howl or whine rather
than bark.

RIGHT:

**Atlantic puffin, Troms og
Finnmark, Norway**
In spring, the Atlantic puffin
breeds on the Arctic coasts of
Russia, Scandinavia, Iceland,
Greenland and Canada, as
well as around the northern
Atlantic Ocean. Similar to
other members of the auk
family, puffins are high-speed
underwater swimmers, diving
deep to capture such fish as
cod and herring.

LEFT:

Eurasian elk bull, Lapland, Sweden

Known in North America as moose, *Alces alces* is the largest member of the deer family. The Eurasian elk subspecies is found from Norway to northern Russia. Only males grow antlers, their size and symmetry reflecting the animal's age and health. With a single lobe on each side, the antlers have a shape reminiscent of a seashell. Females select a mate according to antler size.

BELOW:

Eurasian elk mother and calf, Lapland, Sweden

Unlike other deer, elk are solitary animals, apart from mothers and calves, which remain together until not long before the mother is due to give birth again. Calves are born in May or June, ready for the warmest summer months. Young elk and weakened adults are at risk of attack by brown bears, wolverines and, in parts of their range, wolves.

LEFT:

Northern red-backed vole, Chukotka, Russia

These small voles live in taiga, shrubland and tundra through Alaska, continental Canada, Scandinavia and northern Asia. During the winter, they construct long tunnels under the snow and use layers of moss for warmth. Northern red-backed voles eat berries, as well as leaves, mosses, lichens and insects.

RIGHT:

European roe deer, Norway

The range of the European roe deer extends from just north of the Arctic Circle to as far south as Iran. After mating in July, when females are in peak condition, fertilized eggs float in the female's uterus for five months before implanting, a reproductive strategy known as delayed implantation. Without the demands of feeding a growing baby, females have sufficient reserves to last through the winter period, when food is scarcer. Kids are born in late May, when warmer weather gives them a good chance of survival.

ABOVE:

Arctic fox in winter, Nunavut, Canada
The Arctic fox lives throughout the Arctic Circle's tundra regions. To conserve body heat, it has short legs, muzzle and ears, as well as a rounded, compact body. This fox's pelage (the coat of a mammal) is dense and multilayered, while its foot pads are also covered in fur. The Arctic fox's diet is based on voles, lemmings, hares, birds and their eggs, as well as carrion.

RIGHT:

Arctic fox in summer, Greenland
More than 90 per cent of the Arctic fox population has seasonal camouflage, with an almost completely white pelage in winter, turning brown and grey in summer. Due to a different allele (one of two or more versions of a gene), the rest of the population stays dark blue, brown or grey throughout the year, but becomes a little paler during winter.

LEFT:

North American brown bear, Yukon, Canada
Adult male 'grizzlies' can weigh up to 360kg (790lb). On average, a grizzly measures about 2m (6.5ft) long. Fur is usually brown with darker legs and pale-tipped fur on the flanks and back. This subspecies of the brown bear lives in Alaska and western Canada, with small populations in Montana, Wyoming and Idaho in the lower 48 states of the USA.

RIGHT:

Barren-ground caribou, Northwest Territories, Canada
This subspecies of reindeer, known as caribou in North America, lives on the tundra of western Greenland and northern Canada, where it eats lichens, sedges, grasses, twigs and mushrooms. Climate change, causing increased rain in the winter, is affecting the caribou's main food source, lichen, which is becoming less nutritious and is often imprisoned under layers of ice.

**Snowy owl,
Manitoba, Canada**
In summer, the snowy owl
nests on a mound or boulder
on the Arctic tundra of
North America or Eurasia.
In winter, it flies up to
3000km (1800 miles)
southward. This is one of
the largest owl species, with
a wingspan up to 1.5m (5ft)
wide. Feeding mostly on
lemmings, voles and juvenile
birds, the snowy owl swallows
its prey whole, regurgitating
the bones, teeth, fur or
feathers 18 to 24 hours later.

LEFT:
Canada lynx, Northwest Territories, Canada
Thick fur and broad paws allow this lynx to weather the cold
and soft snow of the Alaskan and Canadian taiga, from the
treeline to just south of the border with the lower 48 states.
Although this lynx can be spotted during the day, it tends to be
nocturnal, like its favoured prey, the snowshoe hare.

ABOVE:
Wolverine, Lapland, Finland
This stocky, sharp-toothed mustelid, up to 107cm (42in) long,
can kill prey much larger than itself, such as deer, bison and
elk (or moose). Smaller prey includes Canada lynx, lemmings
and moles. The wolverine's main predator is the grey wolf,
against which it will put up a tremendous fight.

RIGHT:

Willow ptarmigan, Troms og Finnmark, Norway

With his wattles flushed bright red to attract a female, this willow ptarmigan is in his spring mating plumage. In summer, he will be completely brown, before turning entirely white for winter. During summer, this bird feeds on berries, flowers and seeds, but in winter he may subsist on twigs.

FAR RIGHT:

Arctic terns and black-legged kittiwakes, Svalbard archipelago, Norway

Arctic terns have the longest migrations of any bird, with circuitous return trips of 90,000km (56,000 miles) for some populations. Arctic terns see two summers each year, breeding around the coasts of the Arctic Ocean and northern Atlantic and Pacific oceans during the northern summer, then spending the southern summer over the Southern Ocean. Black-legged kittiwakes have a similar breeding range, but winter sees them only as far south as the northern Pacific and Atlantic oceans.

LEFT:

European viper, Sweden
Found farther north than any
other snake, the European
viper (or common adder)
is seen from Scandinavia's
Arctic Circle to Greece. It
eats birds, lizards, frogs, voles
and invertebrates. In the far
north of its range, the viper
hibernates for eight months.

ABOVE:

**Arctic ground squirrel,
Yukon, Canada**
This ground squirrel lives in
Arctic and subarctic North
America and northeastern
Russia. During at least six
months of the winter, it
hibernates in its food-stocked
burrow, which is lined with
lichen, leaves and muskox hair.

ABOVE RIGHT:

Eurasian lynx, Finland
With a vast range, from
Norway to China and
the Arctic Circle to the
Himalayas, this large lynx is
found in taiga and steppe. It
may hunt over vast areas, up
to 450 sq km (175 sq miles),
searching for hares, rabbits,
deer and reindeer.

**Snowshoe hare,
Alaska, USA**

Named for its wide, furry-
soled feet, which prevent
it sinking into soft snow,
the snowshoe hare lives
in Alaska, Canada and
the Rocky Mountains and
Appalachians of the lower 48
states. It does not hibernate,
its fur changing from brown
to white in winter for
camouflage against the snow.

Muskox, Nunavut, Canada

Found mainly in the
Canadian Arctic and
Greenland, the muskox
stands up to 1.5m (5ft) tall
at the shoulder. Both males
and females have long, curved
horns. The muskox's thick,
streaked coat has long guard
hairs that reach almost to the
ground. The wool, known in
Inuktitut as *qiviut*, is prized
for its softness and warmth.
This species is named for
the strong odour emitted by
males in the mating season.

Narwhals, Baffin Island, Nunavut, Canada
Native to the Arctic Ocean, the narwhal is a toothed whale. It feeds mostly on flatfish, diving to the seafloor for them, beneath the sea ice. During winter, these whales are usually found in family or social groups of five to 20, but in summer they may come together in groups of up to a thousand.

RIGHT:

Narwhal, Nunavut, Canada

The narwhal's tusk is actually a canine tooth, which grows from the left upper jaw, through the whale's lip. It forms a corkscrewing spiral. All males have a tusk that grows throughout their life, reaching up to 3.1m (10.2ft) long. It is possible, though rare, for a male to have a second tusk, when its right-hand canine also grows through the lip. Around one in ten females grows a tusk, not usually as long as a male's.

FAR RIGHT:

Orca, Canada

The world's largest dolphin, up to 8m (26ft) long, the orca is found in all oceans, but is not usually seen in the Arctic Ocean during winter. Global warming, however, is causing the orca's range to extend further into the Arctic and for more of the year. This apex predator, which often hunts in a group, may prey on whales, seals, gulls and fish.

Orca, Russia

The orca's dorsal fin is up to 1.8m (5.9ft) tall, with males having fins twice the height of those of females. This dolphin's large size and strength allow it to reach a top swimming speed of 56km/h (35mph). To conserve oxygen when diving, the orca's heartbeat drops from around 60 beats per minute to 30. It can dive to more than 100m (330ft).

FAR LEFT:

Dall sheep, Alaska, USA
This sheep lives wild in the mountains of Alaska and western Canada. It stays among rocky ridges and steep slopes, where less sure-footed predators cannot follow. Males, which reach 1.4m (4.6ft) long, have thicker, curlier horns than females. During winter, these sheep survive on patches of lichen, moss and frozen grass, where the snow has blown or fallen away.

LEFT:

Fritillary butterfly, Chukotka, Russia
A butterfly feeds on Labrador tea, also known as wild rosemary, which grows widely on the moss and lichen tundra. Of all the world's 17,500 species of butterflies, only a few dozen are found within the Arctic Circle, few of them in the High Arctic. Butterflies can often be seen basking on warm summer days, absorbing heat through their wings.

LEFT:

Wood frog, Alaska, USA
The only North American frog found north of the Arctic Circle, the wood frog enters winter dormancy in surface soil or leaf litter, where it can survive with up to 65 per cent of its body fluids frozen. In preparation for winter, the frog's body accumulates urea and glucose, which act like antifreeze. This species breeds in freshwater pools, usually in forest or woodland.

RIGHT:

Viviparous lizard, Finland
Found further north than any other reptile, this lizard lives from Finland to Spain and Ireland to China. It is named for the fact that northern populations are viviparous, or give birth to live young, rather than laying eggs, as most lizards do. This adaptation increases the chances of successful reproduction in a cold climate. Northern populations also hibernate during winter.

LEFT:

Arctic wolves, Nunavut, Canada

Living north of the tree-line, on Canada's Queen Elizabeth Islands, the Arctic wolf is a subspecies of the grey wolf. This wolf preys on muskoxen, as well as smaller mammals, beetles and birds. Since these wolves rarely get the chance to see people, they are unafraid when they do come across humans and may approach cautiously.

ABOVE:

Siberian brown lemming, Wrangel Island, Russia

This rodent does not hibernate, but often shelters in its burrow under the snow. It feeds on plant materials, such as grass, moss and berries, while watching for snowy owls and Arctic foxes. The lemming population is known for its dramatic fluctuations, caused by overpopulation followed by depletion of resources.

LEFT:

Gyrfalcon, Alaska, USA
The gyrfalcon breeds on
Arctic islands and coasts in
North America and Eurasia.
As temperatures rise, the
gyrfalcon is being driven
further north by the arrival of
peregrine falcons. It has been
seen resting on sea ice far
from land. The gyrfalcon's
avian prey ranges from
ptarmigans to gulls, while
mammals include shrews,
ground squirrels and bats.
Female gyrfalcons, which
are larger than males,
have wingspans of up to
1.6m (5.3ft).

RIGHT:

**Alaskan tundra wolf,
Alaska, USA**
Found only in the tundra
of the northern Alaskan
coast, this subspecies of
the grey wolf measures up
to 1.6m (5.3ft) from nose
to tip of tail. Its favoured
prey is deer, but it will also
feed on smaller mammals,
such as hares. Only the
dominant male and female
of each pack breed, with the
female giving birth to around
four pups, which will be
raised communally.

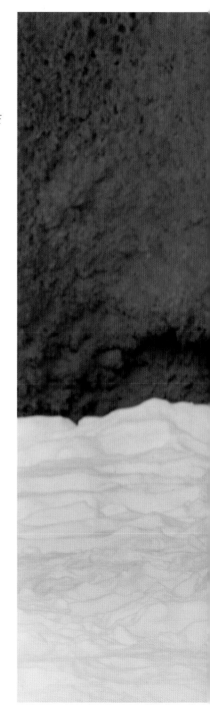

LEFT:

Red fox, Chukotka, Russia
The red fox is found from North Africa to the Arctic Circle of both Eurasia and North America, but is absent from the Arctic islands and Greenland. This species is an opportunistic omnivore, eating countless small animal species as well as fruits, nuts and grasses. With its larger build, this species dominates other foxes. The Arctic fox lives only to the north of the red fox's widening range to avoid competition.

RIGHT:

Mountain reindeer, Troms og Finnmark, Norway
Norway's population of wild mountain reindeer numbers around 80,000. Weighing up to 150kg (330lb), this reindeer has few predators, but attacks by lynx, wolverines, brown bears and occasionally wolves are not unknown. The mountain reindeer's winter coat is cream to pale brown, while its summer coat is darker brown.

Svalbard reindeer, Svalbard archipelago, Norway

Found only on the Svalbard archipelago, this reindeer is much smaller than other subspecies, weighing up to 90kg (200lb). To conserve heat in the harsh climate of the far north, it also has shorter legs, a smaller head and thicker fur than other reindeer. This species is very sedentary, a behaviour that allows it to spend the winter mostly living off its own fat reserves. The Svalbard reindeer is found on nearly all the archipelago's unglaciated land, feeding on shrubs, sedges and grasses.

Snow goose, Canada

This goose breeds on the tundra along the Arctic coasts of Alaska, Canada, Greenland and the northeastern tip of Russia. In winter, it flies southward on narrow migration corridors up to 4800km (3000 miles) long. The head of a snow goose may be stained a rusty shade by minerals in the waterlogged soil where it frequently eats. Its diet includes aquatic plants, grasses, willows, horsetails and grain that has been left behind in farmers' fields.

**Male walrus, Svalbard
archipelago, Norway**
The walrus swims in the
coastal waters of the Arctic
Ocean and the far north
of the Atlantic and Pacific
oceans, where it hunts for
bottom-dwelling shellfish.
Both male and female
walruses grow tusks, which
can reach 1m (3.3ft) long.
Tusks are used for making
holes in the sea ice and for
hauling these large mammals
out of the water on to
slippery ice. Males also
use their tusks for fighting
and display.

RIGHT:

**Walruses, Poolepynten, Prins
Karls Forland, Svalbard
archipelago, Norway**
The headland of Poolepynten
is home to a large walrus
colony. In summer, males
spend long hours lying
on the beach here as their
hair moults. Walrus skin is
particularly tough and up
to 4cm (1.6in) thick. Males
have their thickest skin on
their neck and shoulders as
protection against the tusk
jabs of rival males.

LEFT:

**Hoary marmot,
Yukon, Canada**
A large ground squirrel, the
hoary marmot is also known
as the whistle pig, due to its
high-pitched warning call to
other members of its colony.
'Hoary' describes the silver
fur on its shoulders and
upper back.

OPPOSITE TOP LEFT:

Mountain hare, Russia
Sporting an almost
completely white pelage in
winter, the mountain hare
moults to brown for summer,
but keeps its white tail. The
mountain hare does not dig a
burrow, instead sheltering in
dips in the ground or snow
called 'forms'.

OPPOSITE BOTTOM LEFT:

Tundra vole, Alaska, USA
The range of the tundra vole
stretches from northwestern
Canada, through Alaska and
northern Asia to Scandinavia.
In winter, this vole tunnels
through the snow, while in
summer it tramples runways
through the grass while
hunting for seeds and roots to
store in its burrow.

FAR RIGHT:

Harp seal, Greenland
Harp seal pups are born with
a pure white coat, which
starts to darken from their
first moult. To cope with the
glare of the sun reflecting
off the sea ice, these seals
have eyes with highly mobile
pupils that contract rapidly.

Living in the Arctic

The Arctic has probably been inhabited for around 20,000 years. Today, the region is home to about four million people, 10 per cent of them self-identifying as belonging to an indigenous group. Indigenous Arctic societies include, among many others, the Inupiat and Gwich'in in Alaska; Inuit in Canada and Greenland; Sámi in northern Scandinavia and western Russia; and Nenets, Khanty, Dolgan and Chukchi in Russia. All of these groups adapted to the harsh climate and sparse resources of the Arctic, not just with their clothing, modes of transport and styles of shelter, but also through their social bonds, stories and outlook. Since agriculture is impossible in most of the Arctic, they survived through fishing, hunting, herding and gathering wild plants.

Over the millennia, the Arctic has seen many new arrivals, some brief visitors and others who put down permanent roots. Vikings settled in Greenland around a thousand years ago. During the Age of Exploration, European adventurers, whalers and merchants pushed to the north. Along the coasts, trading posts and ports grew. Today, although some inhabitants of the Arctic still choose to live as their ancestors have for hundreds or thousands of years, many reside in towns and cities. Those who follow a traditional lifestyle, as well as many town-dwellers, are facing existential threats from climate change, industrialization and globalization. As a result, most indigenous groups have organized politically to defend their land, their culture and their rights to resources.

LEFT:
Saqqaq, Greenland
On the coast of west Greenland, Saqqaq has around 190 inhabitants. Excavations in the locality have uncovered remains of the so-called Saqqaq culture, which was based here from c. 2500 BC to 800 BC. DNA sequencing on the frozen remains of a local man, who lived around 2000 BC, showed he was related to the indigenous groups of northeastern Russia.

LEFT:

Abandoned cabin, Troms og Finnmark, Norway

For 3500 years, the Sámi have lived in Norway's far north, part of the Sápmi cultural region that stretches through northern Norway, Sweden, Finland and western Russia. Traditionally, the Sámi lived by semi-nomadic reindeer herding, fishing and trapping. Today, only around 10 per cent of them are involved in reindeer husbandry, while many live in towns and cities in Sápmi and elsewhere. Keeping alive the Sámi language and culture, however, including the singing of *yoik* song-chants and carving with antlers and bone, is of vital importance to many Sámi.

RIGHT:

Reindeer marking, Troms og Finnmark, Norway

Each summer, Sámi reindeer herders must ear-mark each of their new calves. The calves, born in May, are first gathered into a corral. Using a knife, the herder carves their family mark, passed down over many generations. Today, in Norway and Sweden, reindeer husbandry is legally protected as an exclusively Sámi livelihood, so only people with a link to a Sámi herding family can own reindeer.

FAR LEFT:

Reindeer herding, Chukotka, Russia

The Chukchi are the indigenous inhabitants of the Chukchi Peninsula in Russia's far east. Today, around 16,000 people who identify as Chukchi live in the region and across the world. The coastal Chukchi traditionally subsisted by hunting whales and seals, but on the inland tundra, reindeer herding was their primary means of survival.

LEFT:

Moving camp, Taymyr Peninsula, Russia

The majority of Dolgan people live on the Taymyr Peninsula, in the far north of central Russia. Traditionally, the Dolgans were nomadic reindeer herders and hunters. During the Soviet era, their nomadic lifestyle was curtailed, yet today some pursue the old way of life, moving their portable homes, known as *baloks*, between pastures. Lightweight wooden *baloks*, containing wood stoves, are built on runners.

Blizzard, Nunavut, Canada

Blizzards are a frequent occurrence during the Arctic winter, with the chance of sudden storms receding only at the height of summer. The lifestyle and culture of Arctic indigenous societies is adapted to such extreme conditions, while more recent inhabitants of the region have been led by their example. For all long-term residents of the Arctic, modern insulating fabrics, heating systems and transport are welcomed as a benefit rather than as a replacement for planning and stoicism.

Troms og Finnmark, Norway

A thermometer shows -12°C (10°F) outside a Norwegian cabin. The Sápmi region's vast, tundra-covered Finnmarksvidda plateau has a continental climate, registering the coldest winter temperatures in the whole of Norway: -51.4°C (-60.5°F). The area has an extremely low population density, of around 1.55 people per one sq km (four people per one sq mile).

Yaranga, Chukotka, Russia
A Chukchi *yaranga* is similar in structure to a Mongolian yurt. A *yaranga* consists of a light, circular wooden frame, driven firmly into the ground and covered with reindeer skins. To form the roof, slim poles are bundled together by horizontal rings. Since a *yaranga* is hard to warm, a smaller enclosure, in which the family are doubly insulated, is built inside.

LEFT:

Fishing for salmon, Tiniteqilaaq, Greenland

Traditionally, the Greenlandic Inuit diet includes only those foods that can be fished, hunted or gathered locally. This led to a diet high in protein and fat, but low in carbohydrate. Grasses, roots, berries and seaweed were the only plant matter. Since around 1980, when imported or greenhouse-grown foods became more widely available, the Greenlandic diet has been more varied, particularly in Nuuk and other large towns.

RIGHT:

Fish traps, Sisimiut, Greenland

Around 6800 Greenlanders, or 12 per cent of the population, are employed in fishing, many of them aboard about 300 registered fishing vessels. Every year, the port of Sisimiut brings in around 20,000 tons of shrimp, as well as salmon, halibut and cod.

FAR RIGHT:

Drying salmon, Alaska, USA

Across much of the Arctic region, fish is dried by cold air and the wind. Wooden drying racks are often erected on the foreshore. This method of food preservation, probably the world's oldest, removes the water that bacteria, yeasts and moulds need to grow. Once dried, fish can last for several years and are easily transported.

Whaling camp on the Chukchi Sea, Alaska, USA
In line with indigenous rights to sustainable whaling, Inupiat hunters spend the spring waiting on the shore, watching for bowhead whales migrating north from the Bering Sea. When a whale is spotted, a whaling crew pushes a wooden-frame, hide-covered boat, called an *umiak*, on to the water. When a whale is successfully harpooned, the meat is shared between the crew and the wider community.

Ilulissat harbour, Greenland
During the coldest months of
winter, the fishing harbour
at Ilulissat, on Disko Bay,
is imprisoned by sea ice.
Disko Bay is the centre of
Greenland's fishing industry,
which is the mainstay of the
economy, accounting for
more than 90 per cent of
exports. The port's biggest
catches are Greenland
halibut, cold-water shrimp
and cod.

FAR RIGHT:

**Henningsvær, Lofoten
Islands, Norway**
The fishing village of
Henningsvær is scattered
across several islets, including
Heimøya and Hellandsøya,
connected by bridge to the
larger island of Austvågøya.
Before the advent of tourism,
life here centred on fishing,
which remains a major
employer. Banks of wooden
racks for drying cod take up
all available open space.

Tuktoyaktuk, Northwest Territories, Canada
On the shores of the Beaufort Sea is the fishing village of Tuktoyaktuk. Many of its 900 inhabitants identify as Inuvialuit. Most make their living from fishing, tourism, oil, caribou herding or the seasonal trapping of ducks and geese. Known for a while as Port Brabant, Tuktoyaktuk was Canada's first settlement to revert to its traditional name in 1950.

Ilulissat, Greenland
With around 4600 inhabitants, Ilulissat is Greenland's third largest city, after the capital, Nuuk, and the port of Sisimiut. Established on the site of a Kalaallit settlement, Ilulissat became a Danish trading post in 1741, named Jakobshavn after Jacob Severin, the Danish merchant who held a trade monopoly on Greenland. The city has been renamed after the Kalaallisut word for iceberg.

LEFT:

Fishing in Baker Lake, Nunavut, Canada

Baker Lake is home to several Inuit groups, including the Harvaqtuurmiut and Ihalmiut. Most local people make a living from mining or tourism, but some still practise ice fishing and may give demonstrations using traditional equipment. During winter, holes are carved in the lake's ice, then fish are snared with lines, nets or three-pronged spears.

RIGHT:

Igloo building, Canada

Igloos are temporary or semi-permanent houses built of snow, traditionally only by people of Canada's Central Arctic and Greenland's Thule area. The snow from an igloo must be taken from a deep drift, where it has been compacted hard. It is carved into blocks with a snow knife, originally made of bone but today more likely to be metal. An entrance tunnel may be used for storage as well as to reduce wind and heat loss when the sealskin inner door is opened. A slab of clear ice can be used as a window.

BELOW:

Making cord, Uelen, Chukotka, Russia

The village of Uelen is found where the Bering Sea meets the Chukchi Sea. The majority of villagers identify as Chukchi, while others are Yupik or Russian. Here walrus gut is made into tough cord, while walrus ivory is carved into delicate statues, jewellery and utensils.

RIGHT:

Assembling *chums*, Nenets Autonomous Okrug, Russia

Komi reindeer herders assemble their *chums* over their belongings. A *chum* has a design similar to a North American tipi, with reindeer hides draped over wooden poles organized in a circle. Smoke from the central fireplace escapes through a hole at the top of the *chum*.

RIGHT:

Nenets *chums*, Yamal Peninsula, Russia

With its wide base, the Nenets *chum* is stable in the high winds that blow over the vast tundra of the Yamal Peninsula. In Nenets, Yamal means 'end of the land'. The peninsula is home to around 500,000 reindeer owned by Nenets and Khanty herders. Every year, the herders migrate thousands of kilometres. Using lassoes and dogs to carry their belongings by sled, the Nenets herd their reindeer from summer pastures in the north to winter ones south of the Arctic Circle.

FAR RIGHT:

Inside a *balok*, Syndassko, Taymyr Peninsula, Russia

The village of Syndassko is in Taymyria, around 700km (430 miles) north of the Arctic Circle. Inside a Dolgan *balok* home, insulated with reindeer skins, there are two or three beds, a table and a wood stove. During the coldest winter months, the stove rarely heats the hut above 15°C (59°F).

Longyearbyen, Spitsbergen, Svalbard archipelago, Norway
Most housing in the town of Longyearbyen is owned by the Norwegian Government, the university or the mining company Store Norske. Privately funded construction is rare because of strict zoning rules and the risk of avalanches outside the town centre. The average inhabitant of Longyearbyen lives there for only 6.3 years, with 70 per cent of households consisting of a single person.

LEFT:
Inuksuk, Manitoba, Canada
Inuksuit markers are built by the Inuit, Inupiat, Kalaallit, Yupik and other societies of Arctic North America. Cross-shaped *inuksuit* may have appeared after Christian missionaries first visited the region. Some *inuksuit* resemble human figures, with two legs and arms open. These may have been erected to frighten caribou toward their hunters.

ABOVE:
Khanty reindeer camp, Yamalia, Russia
The Khanty live on the West Siberian Plain, from the steppe in the south, through the taiga belt, to the tundra of the north. Traditionally, the Khanty were reindeer herders, fishermen, and hunters and trappers. Today, there are around 30,000 people who identify as Khanty, around a third of them speaking the Khanty language, which is related to Hungarian and Finnish.

Nuuk, Greenland
Greenland's capital has 18,000 residents, almost a third of the island's population. This spot was first occupied by people of the Saqqaq culture in around 2200 BC. It was later inhabited by Vikings, Inuits and Dano-Norwegians. Today, it is home to people who identify as Inuit, Danish, Greenlandic or a mixture of the three, as well as more recent arrivals from around the world.

Wooden snowshoes, Canada
Many of the indigenous
groups of northern
North America developed
snowshoes, with distinct
styles to suit the terrain and
climate. The Inuit used their
snowshoes less than the
people to the south, such
as the Huron (pictured), as
the Inuit did most of their
winter travel on sea ice or
by sled. When they did use
snowshoes, they were often
in the shape of a bear's paw,
reflecting the need to walk
through deep, powdery snow.

**Travelling by sled, Yamal
Peninsula, Russia**
The sled is central to the
life of Nenets herders,
allowing them to travel vast
distances as they move their
reindeer between winter
and summer grounds. While
reindeer or Samoyed dogs are
traditionally used for power,
today some herders use
snow motorcycles. Draught
reindeer are directed using a
long pole called a *khorei*.

Nenets sleds, Yamal Peninsula, Russia

The Nenets make their sleds from lightweight larchwood. Even today, they are crafted using reindeer sinew and bone, without nails or other metal. Everything the family needs is packed into wooden chests. When it is time to set off, sleds carrying children are roped together into a train called an *argysh*.

Nenets tools, Yamal Peninsula, Russia

Knives, chisels and mallets are carried for sled-building and mending. These tools are made from wood and reindeer bone, although plastic and metal may make an appearance. Lassoes are crafted from reindeer tendons, while harnesses may be made from the mammoth tusks that are occasionally discovered.

Qamutiik sled, Nunavut, Canada

A *qamutiik* is designed to travel over both snow and sea ice. It is made without nails or pins: instead, each piece is tied to the next, giving a flexibility that can withstand the pounding of ice travel. Today, wooden runners have replaced walrus ivory, whale bone, antlers or frozen fish wrapped in skins.

BELOW:

Maniitsoq, Greenland

With around 2600 inhabitants, Maniitsoq, along with other small Greenlandic towns, is experiencing slow population decline. With good education but few employment opportunities, many young Greenlanders move to larger, more industrialized towns, to Nuuk or to mainland Denmark. Today, around a quarter of all Greenlanders live abroad.

RIGHT:

Dogsled team, Baffin Bay, Greenland

An Inuit hunter and his dogsled team cross the sea ice in search of seals and walruses. Hunting is central to Greenlandic life, as only around one per cent of the land is arable, even with rising temperatures creating a longer, warmer growing season. However, hunting is threatened by the same rising temperatures, which are dangerously thinning the sea ice.

Tourism, Industry and Research

Despite the Arctic making up eight per cent of the earth's surface, economic exploitation of its resources has, so far, been limited. Since their first arrival in the region, Arctic inhabitants have made use of the area's key biological renewable resources: fish and reindeer. For centuries, these industries were limited mostly to subsistence, but the twentieth century saw the unfettered growth of commercial fishing across the region, followed by a decline as overfishing took its toll. Over the last half-century, discoveries of hydrocarbons, minerals and diamonds have brought new jobs and many newcomers to the Arctic. The desire to exploit these finite natural resources faces pushback from environmentalists and both indigenous and more recent Arctic societies.

In 1882–83, the first International Polar Year was organized, during which Arctic stations, belonging to nine European countries and the United States, took observations and shared results. While this was by no means the start of scientific research in the region, it was an important moment for international collaboration. Today, internationally funded research ranges from studies of the magnetosphere to analysis of climate change. Another rapidly growing industry is tourism, now providing thousands of jobs across the region, although many are seasonal. The challenge over the next decade will be to ensure that the tourist industry both employs and benefits local people – and that its efforts and revenues are channelled into protecting the fragile, beautiful environment it relies on.

LEFT:
Kayaking, Scoresby Sound, Greenland
Travellers kayak through Scoresby Sound, the world's longest fjord system, which branches tree-like into Greenland's southeastern corner. The crack and splash of calving glaciers is a constant soundtrack here. During the long summer days, narwhals can be seen gliding through the water, along with the occasional minke or fin whale.

Trans-Alaska Pipeline, North Slope, Alaska, USA
The Trans-Alaska Pipeline carries oil 1287km (800 miles) from the Prudhoe Bay oilfield, 400km (250 miles) north of the Arctic Circle, to the port of Valdez, in southern Alaska. The waters around Valdez do not freeze in winter, making it the northernmost ice-free port in North America. Since the first barrel of oil was pumped through the pipeline in 1977, over 18 billion have been shipped.

LEFT:

Badami oil field, North Slope, Alaska, USA

Oil was discovered at Badami in 1990, with production beginning in 1998. The North Slope was once a seabed, its long-dead creatures providing all the region's oil. The Badami pipeline connects with the Trans-Alaska Pipeline, around 48km (30 miles) to the west. Badami is a challenging reservoir with variable oil quality, resulting in full and partial shutdowns.

BELOW:

Pumping stations, Prudhoe Bay, Alaska, USA

The Prudhoe Bay oil field, the largest in North America, was discovered in 1967. Production did not get underway until 1977, with the completion of the Trans-Alaska Pipeline. The field's peak of production, in 1989, was two million barrels per day. The nearby settlements of Prudhoe Bay and Deadhorse developed to house and serve the oil field's workers.

Cruise ship, Alaska, USA
Tourism to the Arctic has risen dramatically in the twenty-first century, with up to one million people visiting the region annually by 2019. Local people and international conservation organizations are working with many tour operators to ensure Arctic travel is responsible. In addition to protecting wildlife and the delicate local environment, their collaborations aim to ensure that tourism brings money to local communities without engulfing them.

BELOW:

Hope Bay aerodrome, Nunavut, Canada

The runway at Hope Bay serves the gold mines and exploration camps of the Hope Bay greenstone belt. Mining is a major source of income in Nunavut. In addition to gold, the territory has reserves of diamonds, uranium, nickel, lead, copper, silver, zinc and iron ore, most of them still unexploited.

RIGHT:

Doris Camp, Nunavut, Canada

The Hope Bay greenstone belt contains three large gold deposits, named Doris, Boston and Madrid. In 2017, the Doris North mine was the first to start commercial operations. Canada is the world's fifth largest gold-producing country, after China, Australia, Russia and the United States.

Tanker, Hope Bay, Nunavut, Canada
A tanker delivers fuel for the winter at Hope Bay's gold mines. The mining company has worked closely with local communities, focusing particularly on training for college-educated young people who might otherwise have migrated southward. More than 2000 people in Nunavut are employed in mineral extraction and related support services.

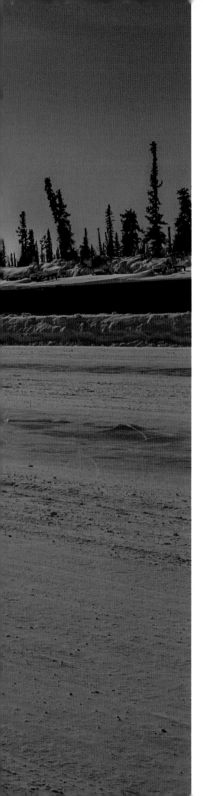

Ice road, Northwest Territories, Canada
In 2017, Canada's most famous ice road, between Inuvik and Tuktoyaktuk, closed after the building of a highway. Several other ice roads remain in use during winter, linking isolated settlements, such as Aklavik, along the streams of the Mackenzie Delta. After thaw, Aklavik is reached only by air.

Icebreaker off the coast of Utqiagvik, Alaska, USA
Utqiagvik, formerly known as Barrow, is the largest city of the North Slope. No roads link Utqiagvik with the rest of Alaska, while its city streets are unpaved due to the permafrost. Transport is via passenger and cargo planes, as well as marine barges during the annual summer and early autumn sealift.

Qamutiik excursion, Baffin Island, Nunavut, Canada
Pulled by snowmobiles rather than a dog team, travellers ride
in _qamutiik_ sleds over the sea ice of Sirmilik National Park's
Oliver Sound. Baffin Island draws the most visitors to Nunavut
every year, due to its winter sports, wildlife-viewing and many
festivals, featuring film, music and theatre.

Krossfjord, Spitsbergen, Svalbard archipelago, Norway
Barrels have been left to rust by Krossfjord since World War
II, when Allied forces were stationed on Spitsbergen to prevent
Nazi Germany from occupying the islands. In 1943, during
the German Operation Zitronella, six Norwegians and one
German soldier were killed.

LEFT:

Dog kennels, Longyearbyen, Spitsbergen, Norway
This kennels runs sledding trips and introduces young visitors to sled dogs of all ages. The dogs are an unusual mix of husky and the Greenland dog, bred in Greenland for stamina over the last 4000 years.

ABOVE:

Port of Barentsburg, Spitsbergen, Norway
Svalbard's second-largest settlement is the Russian coal-mining town of Barentsburg, home to around 470 Russians and Ukrainians. Food is delivered from Russia, but has been supplemented by Longyearbyen in emergencies.

EISCAT Svalbard Radar, Spitsbergen, Norway
The EISCAT (European Incoherent Scatter Scientific Association) operates one of its four Scandinavian radar stations near Longyearbyen. It monitors disturbances in the earth's upper atmosphere, the ionosphere, and in the magnetosphere, the region of space affected by the planet's magnetic field. Such studies shed light on the interaction between the sun and earth.

LEFT:

Kinnvika, Nordaustlandet, Svalbard archipelago, Norway

A rusting sundial is found at the abandoned Swedish-Finnish research station of Kinnvika, built in 1957–59. The station was reopened in 2007–09 to study climate change in the Arctic. Even the complex's sauna, probably the most northerly sauna in the world, was cleaned up and put to good use.

RIGHT:

Automatic weather station, Spitsbergen, Svalbard archipelago, Norway

Positioned on the Nordenskiöld glacier, this automatic station monitors wind, temperature, humidity, air pressure, radiation and snow depth. In addition, instruments take note of the ice velocity of the glacier itself. The first permanent weather station was established on the Svalbard archipelago in 1911.

ALL PHOTOGRAPHS:

Pyramiden, Spitsbergen, Svalbard archipelago, Norway
The Russian coal-mining settlement of Pyramiden was
abandoned after the last coal was extracted, on 31 March 1998.
Between 1910 and 1998, Pyramiden had over 1000 inhabitants,
a primary school, sports centre, theatre, library and hotel.
Today, the hotel at the centre of the ghost town has reopened
under the management of the Arktikugol mining company.

Petrol station, Longyearbyen, Spitsbergen, Norway
Longyearbyen is home to the world's most northerly petrol station, as well as the northernmost car-rental office, taxi rank, bus station and airport with scheduled flights. Other useful record-breaking facilities for travellers and the town's 2370 inhabitants include a police station, bookshop, toy shop, supermarket, library and ATM.

Disused cablecar station, Longyearbyen, Spitsbergen, Norway
Known locally as Taubanesentrale, this abandoned cablecar station was used for transporting coal from 1956 until 1987. There were once numerous coal mines in this area, but today only one remains, with its coal transported by truck from Adventdalen, around 15km (9 miles) away, to Longyearbyen's harbour.

RIGHT:

Boat trip, Svalbard archipelago, Norway

Travel by boat is one of the best ways to see the Svalbard archipelago's wildlife, such as walruses, whales and seabirds. Day trips departing from Longyearbyen's harbour will pass glacier termini, such as that of Esmarkbreen, and call in at some of the island's other settlements, including Ny-Ålesund, Barentsburg and the deserted Pyramiden.

FAR RIGHT:

Russian Scientific Centre, Barentsburg, Spitsbergen, Norway

The Russian Scientific Centre coordinates Russia's scientific activities on the archipelago. It incorporates a satellite receiving and transmission station (pictured), a laboratory and a meteorological and geophysical observatory. Up to 100 Russian researchers and students visit the centre during summer, while just a dozen stay through the dark and stormy winter.

ABOVE:

Kakslauttanen Arctic resort, Lapland, Finland
While staying in a glass-roofed igloo for views of the aurora,
visitors to Kakslauttanen can also meet Santa Claus. Lapland
is associated with Santa because of the folklore, popularized
by Finnish children's radio-show host Markus Rautio in 1927,
that he lives on the region's Korvatunturi mountain ('mountain
of the ear'), where he can hear if children are naughty or nice.

RIGHT:

Icebreaker cruise, Bay of Bothnia, Finland
Although it lies south of the Arctic Circle, the Bay of Bothnia
is covered by ice for up to 190 days each year. The bay's low
temperatures and low salinity result in extremely strong ice,
which it is possible to walk on with a guide. From the deck of
an icebreaker, ringed and grey seals may be seen resting on the
ice between dives for crustaceans and fish.

LEFT:

Weather radar station, Luosto, Lapland, Finland
Luosto's weather radar, situated on a fell top, is used to locate and monitor precipitation. In winter, the small resort of Luosto offers skiing, sled rides, Santa Claus visits and clear views of the northern lights. During summer, the forested Phyä-Luosto National Park is popular for hikes under the midnight sun.

RIGHT:

Snowmobile excursion, Saariselkä, Lapland, Finland
From the resort of Saariselkä, hikes or snowmobile rides can be taken in the Urho Kekkonen National Park, one of Finland's largest protected areas. The park was named after Urho Kekkonen, Finland's longest-serving president, who served from 1956 to 1982. Reindeer herding, as well as reindeer racing, are common sources of income in this region.

Aurora Sky Station, Abisko, Lapland, Sweden
Renowned for being an excellent location for viewing the northern lights, the Sky Station is on a fell top in Abisko National Park, where light pollution is far from a problem. Ideally visited between December and March for the best views of the lights, the Sky Station is reached by chair lift from near the shores of the vast Lake Torneträsk.

Exploratory drilling rig, Davis Strait, Greenland
Greenland has potentially immense hydrocarbon wealth, but is far from blind to the irony of contributing to the industry that is melting its own glaciers. Although exploratory drilling has taken place in the waters off Greenland, no commercial drilling has yet begun, a situation that environmentalists would like to see continue.

BELOW:

Arctic Station, Qeqertarsuaq, Disko Island, Greenland
The University of Copenhagen's Arctic Station faces Disko
Bay and its huge icebergs. The facility carries out research
into Arctic environmental issues, including the effect of global
warming on flora and fauna. The facility is outside the town of
Qeqertarsuaq, meaning 'Large Island' in Kalaallisut in reference
to Disko Island's 9700 sq km (3750 sq miles).

RIGHT:

Fishing, Disko Bay, Greenland
Greenland's fishing industry contributes 20 per cent of the
island's gross national income. Most of Greenland's fish and
seafood exports go to Denmark, Iceland, Norway, Germany,
Japan, the UK and USA. The Royal Greenland company,
owned by the Government of Greenland, manages ten
processing plants, where fish are usually placed in frozen cans.

LEFT:

Radome, Nuuk, Greenland

Communications in Greenland are run by the publicly owned
TELE Greenland, which manages the .gl internet domain
and owns the Greenland Connect submarine cables, linking
Greenland, Canada and Iceland. Around 65 per cent of
Greenlanders have internet access, compared with 95 per cent
in Denmark as a whole.

ABOVE:

Filling station, Uummannaq, Greenland

Uummannaq Island, just off Greenland's west coast, is home
to the largest town north of Ilulissat, named Uummannaq.
Most of the island's 1280 inhabitants are fishermen or hunters,
although a growing number are employed in the tourist
industry. There are still 500 sled dogs on Uummannaq, but
there is also a petrol station for cars and snowmobiles.

LEFT:

Dog-sled tour, Tasiilaq, Greenland

Tasiilaq is a growing town on Greenland's east coast, the region where East Greenlandic, or Tunumiit Oraasiat, is spoken. In winter, dog-sledding, snowmobiling, skiing and heliskiing are on offer. The town was the location for the shooting of the first Greenlandic film, *The Wedding of Palo* (1934), which tells the story of two Inuit men competing for the love of a woman, Navarana.

RIGHT:

Icebreaker cruise, Antarctic Haven, Greenland

The bay of Antarctic Haven, in the Northeast Greenland National Park, was named in 1899 by Swedish explorer Alfred Gabriel Nathorst after he moored his ship, *Antarctic*, there while searching for survivors from Salomon August Andrée's ill-fated attempt to reach the North Pole by hydrogen balloon. The world's largest national park, Northeast Greenland can be explored by vessels only during the ice-free summer months.

**Hotel Arctic,
Ilulissat, Greenland**
Greenland's most northerly
four-star hotel offers
two-person igloo cabins
overlooking the Icefjord, for
stays from May to October.
Diners in the hotel restaurant
can enjoy local ingredients,
such as salted muskox heart,
Greenland halibut tartar and
prawns with Greenlandic
thyme. Reindeer steak can be
cut using knives with reindeer
bone handles.

LEFT:

Siglufjörður Harbour, Iceland

On Iceland's north coast, fewer than 40km (25 miles) from the Arctic Circle, is the fishing town of Siglufjörður. The population has been slowly shrinking since the 1950s, alongside the herring catch. From 2015, Siglufjörður gained international fame as the location for the popular television crime drama series *Trapped*, starring Ólafur Darri Ólafsson.

ABOVE:

Fishing in Ísafjörður, Iceland

Historically, fishing has been Ísafjörður's main industry. While fishing still remains central to the local economy, the decline in the fish population has led to inhabitants seeking work elsewhere and a growth in new industries. Tourism, drawn by the Hornstrandir Peninsula nature reserve, is a key area of growth, alongside startups, such as a company that makes fish-skin products to heal wounds.

Kayaking, Vatnajökull National Park, Iceland

Jökulsárlón is a vast glacial lake in the south of Iceland's largest national park, Vatnajökull. Kayakers must paddle their way between seals and the icebergs calved by the Breiðamerkurjökull glacier. During summer, nesting Arctic skuas and Arctic terns can be seen along the shore. For those less willing to get wet, tours of the lake are offered by boat or amphibious vehicle.

Dudinka, Krasnoyarsk Krai, Russia
This port on the Yenisei River docks cargo for the mining towns of Talnakh, Norilsk and Kayerkan, loading it on to the Norilsk Railway. In return, Dudinka receives metal, coal and ore. From the railway's construction, in 1937, until 2010, it was Russia's northernmost line. The record was then taken by the Obskaya–Bovanenkovo Line on the Yamal Peninsula.

Husky kennels, Franz Josef Land, Russia

At the decaying Sedov weather station, on Hooker Island's Tikhaya Bay, are the rotting kennels once used by the meteorologists' huskies. The weather station was in operation from 1929 to 1963. After a hiatus of half a century, meteorological readings restarted on the site in 2012, while visitors from passing cruise ships are invited to take a tour.

LEFT:

Arktichesky Trilistnik, Franz Josef Land, Russia
The Arktichesky Trilistnik ('Arctic Trefoil') military base is on
Alexandra Land, one of the westernmost islands in the Franz
Josef Land Archipelago. Named for its three-lobed shape, the
new base replaced one built in 1947, originally as a staging base
for Soviet Long Range Aviation bombers to reach the United
States. The base is built on stilts to withstand the extreme cold
and houses 150 personnel on 18-month tours of duty.

BELOW:

***Yamal* Russian nuclear icebreaker, Arctic Ocean**
Yamal is an Arktika-class nuclear-powered icebreaker, among
the most powerful icebreakers in the world. The ship carries
travellers to and from the North Pole, departing from the
Russian port of Murmansk and taking in Franz Josef Land
and walks on the pack ice. Whales, walruses and polar bears,
as well as colonies of such seabirds as guillemots, dovekies and
ivory gulls, may be spotted from the deck.

ALL PHOTOGRAPHS:
Abandoned military buildings, Russkaya Gavan, Novaya Zemlya
Most of the Novaya Zemlya archipelago's 2400 inhabitants are Russian military personnel. During the Cold War, the islands were used for nuclear testing, including the air-burst detonation in 1961 of Tsar Bomba, the most powerful nuclear explosion ever detonated. The mushroom cloud was seen from a distance of 160km (100 miles) away.

LEFT:
Glamping, Kola Peninsula, Russia

Despite its Arctic Circle location, the Kola Peninsula experiences unusually mild winter temperatures, averaging -10°C (14°F) in January, due to the Gulf Stream. Tourism, particularly eco-tourism, has been developing on the peninsula in the last decade. In addition to viewing the northern lights, glampers can hike in a wilderness of pine and spruce forest or across tundra of grasses, lichens, cloudberries and dwarf birch.

RIGHT:
Abandoned polar station, Vize Island, Russia

This remote, uninhabited island lies in the Kara Sea, midway between Franz Josef Land and Severnaya Zemlya. Due to battering by Arctic storms, made worse by melting of the sea ice, the island's coastline is receding at an extraordinary rate: up to 74m (243ft) between 2009 and 2016. The island's abandoned clifftop hydrometeorological polar station is currently at vertiginous risk.

Picture Credits